VIRTUE STORIES

Handle with Care

Lalita Iyer

Om KIDZ
An imprint of Om Books International

Ali couldn't wait any more! His mum was on her way home with his baby brother. Ali had met his brother a few days ago. He hadn't been able to visit him again although he badly wanted to. The doctors had given strict instructions that he shouldn't go to the hospital because of his cold. Ali wasn't too upset as he knew all about germs and what they could do, especially to a small baby.

Besides, his baby brother was the bringer of many gifts - a shining red toy truck, a set of dinosaurs and his favourite - a big drum that someone had gifted and Papa kept away on the highest shelf in his room. 'The neighbours will get disturbed,' Papa said by way of explaining, when Ali insisted on using it during nap time, in the afternoon.

Ali knew that it would take a while for the baby to grow up and until then, the gifts were his. He could not wait for his brother to arrive so that he could show him how everything works!

Just then, the
doorbell rang.
It was Mama
with the baby!

Ali ran straight into his Mama's arms. His brother seemed scared of all the noise and began to cry. Mama put him to bed, though not before Ali gave him a tight squeeze, which made him cry louder.

The next day, Ali introduced his best friend Big Mac, the barking dog, to his brother. Big Mac had a soft bark and Ali brought him close to his brother's ear so he could hear him well. But his brother burst out crying and had to be hurriedly carried away again.

Ali tried to cuddle his brother that night - he was looking adorable in his soft rabbit suit. But his grandma lifted his brother out of reach and only let him look at him. That night, Ali was very sad.

When Mama asked him what the matter was, he said that his brother did not like him and always cried when he came near.

Mama said 'hmmm' and looked thoughtful.

'I think it's because he cannot talk and may be, he thinks that you - because you're So big and strong compared to how little and weak he is - could hurt him. So maybe, if we could put up a sign that reminded you of how he felt, you would be more gentle with him?'

'Ok, Mama,' Ali said, his eyes shining brightly. 'But what should we put on the sign?'

Mama thought again. 'A "Handle with care" sign would be perfect!' Ali and Mama tore out some sheets of paper from his scrapbook and Mama drew a big skull and Ali put in a big 'X' all over each sheet. Mama said skulls and Xs were signs to tell us to be careful, though she gave the skull a nice big smiley face!

HANDLE WITH CARE
HANDLE WITH CARE
HANDLE WITH CARE
HANDLE WITH CARE

Then they snuck into his brother's nursery. They put the signs up everywhere with a little bit of sticky tape as a reminder for Ali that he would need to be sensitive to his little brother's needs, even though he didn't have the same needs as the little one. The solution worked wonderfully! In a few days, Ali's brother stopped crying. Ali was around him, and they both started their adventures as brothers and best friends.